HOW TO USE VIRTUAL ASSISTANTS SUCCESSFULLY

BY LAURIE LEIKER

Author of "Help! My Texts and Emails Are Ruining My Life!"

© 2018 Laurie Leiker

To Cris Koenig, Mandy Brown, and Beth Moffat, who taught me what being a Virtual Assistant was all about.

To Lorenzo Gomez, who bore with me during the first days of our relationship, and who became a great friend, as well as my first client.

To Julie Huser and Sarah Atkisson, who bear with me as I go through the various stages of entrepreneurship, as a sister, a daughter, and, mostly, as friends.

Table of Contents

- Introduction
- The Gig Economy
- The 10 Tips
    - Setting expectations on both sides
    - Meetings
    - Contracts
    - Negotiations
    - Payments
- When Things Go Wrong
- Embracing Virtual Assistants in the Gig Economy and the 11th Tip
- About the Author

Introduction

Thank you for choosing "How To Use Virtual Assistants Successfully." This book has been in the works for almost two years, as the world of Virtual Assistants has grown around it.

When I first started working, the thought of someone being able to work at home doing anything other than laundry and cleaning was unimaginable. Women, especially, were told they needed to either work in an office in a clerical capacity or stay home and take care of children and the home.

Over the years, there were legitimate work-from-home jobs, mostly still in the clerical realm, with medical transcription taking the top spot of professions where one could work remotely. Unfortunately, with the improvement in speech-to-text, and the passing of legislation requiring all hospitals and doctor's offices to switch to electronic medical records, the medical transcription profession has become unsupportable.

I spent over a dozen years in the medical transcription field, mostly in management positions, working with strong, intelligent, professional women, all of whom worked from home. They were hard-working and defied every stereotype of being "just a medical transcriptionist." As years passed and the industry changed, it was heartbreaking to see these very intelligent women having to go on food stamps because their work was being overtaken by editing transcripts and their pay going down to sub-sustainable rates.

Fast forward to 2018, when more and more are working remotely, either at home or at a coworking-type location. At the same time, more and more micro and small businesses are popping up and secretarial/assistant jobs are being phased out, leaving business owners and executives having to do their own appointment setting, email answering, and social media postings.

Enter virtual assistants, or VAs. What's a VA? A VA is a highly-trained, professional person who provides everything from email and calendar management to social media strategy and management, website design, creative content, travel coordination, and anything else you can think of. And they work from home, sometimes states and time zones away from where their clients are.

The VA field is brand new. It hasn't been tried before. So this book is dedicated to those hardworking VAs and you, their clients. May the information in this book lead to great VA-client relationships and friendships, with growing businesses on both sides.

- Laurie

The Gig Economy and Virtual Assistants

According to ***Entrepreneur*** magazine, the gig economy -- working remotely, doing a variety of jobs, from driving for Uber or Lyft to being a temporary Chief Finance Officer – is growing by leaps and bounds. In their article dated December 20, 2018, entitled, "*These 4 Business Trends Will Have a Major Impact in 2019 – Watch Them Closely*," the gig economy will continue to grow, as will the trend toward working remotely.

Entrepreneur cites a study by the Federal government showing that as many as 75 million Americans work in some way as part of the gig economy. At the same time, the magazine quotes a ***New York Times*** article from February 2017 showing that as many as 43-percent of employees are working remotely.

While some companies have experimented with remote workers and have failed, returning employees to the office, even more companies are embracing the Gig Economy. Why?

> *"Employees are pushing companies to break down the long-established structures and policies that traditionally have influenced their workdays."*
>
> -- *Niraj Chokshi,*
> "*Out of the Office: More People Are Working Remotely, Survey Finds*,"
> ***New York Times*** *2/15/17*

The Gig Economy and Virtual Assistants

Chances are, you know someone working in the Gig Economy. They may work from home with their own company or work remotely for someone else's company. In fact, you, yourself, may be working remotely.

Regardless of what a person does at home, the statistics bear out that those working remotely are more productive, more engaged, and are generally better employees than those working in an office.

Virtual Assistants fall into that group of people who are very dedicated to their work. They build their businesses around the idea that they can help small and micro businesses be more efficient, market themselves more effectively, and can bring a sense of calm to the chaos that can be owning your own business or working remotely.

> *"Employers who are working on projects or are looking to develop positions no longer have to go through a costly and tedious hiring process. They can focus on specific skill sets and hire for them with time-limited horizons."*
> -- Miles Jennings
> *"7 Reasons Why the Gig Economy is a Net Positive,"* **New York Times** 4/5/18

The 10 Tips

Hiring a Virtual Assistant can be both rewarding and frustrating at the same time. By following these 10 tips, broken down into five categories, you'll make your job of finding a VA easier, and you'll be more likely to get the right VA on the first try.

One of the biggest fallacies about the Gig Economy, and the role of virtual assistants is that you can pay less and still get good quality. That belief is blatantly untrue, regardless of the role for which you are hiring. Getting a VA offshore ends up, most of the time, being more frustrating than most can handle. When it blows up, the hiring person believes VAs are a waste of time and money. Is that so? No. As with most roles in the Gig Economy, you get what you pay for. Literally.

The key to hiring and establishing a good VA that's perfect for you and the job is to follow these 10 tips, by

- Setting expectations, before, during, and after engagement
- Be clear on meetings with your VA
- Getting a written contract and abiding by it
- Negotiating in good faith to get a working relationship that works for both you and your VA
- Establish a payment schedule

In most cases, the VA you're talking to already has some of this in place for his/her business, so you won't have to recreate the wheel. And most professional have an onboarding package that will help clearly define your working relationship. Review this information carefully and, if the VA you're working for doesn't already have a contract or an onboarding system, walk away – they're not ready to be a professional Virtual Assistant.

So here's your top 10 tips for working successfully with a Virtual Assistant, with two tips in the five categories above.

The 10 Tips: Setting Expectations

Setting expectations is essential to any relationship, so setting your expectations for a new Virtual Assistant is crucial. The first two tips for having success with your Virtual Assistant have to do with setting expectations.

1. Know your "why" clearly

Why do you want a Virtual Assistant? Is it because you're feeling overloaded? Are you missing meetings and emails because you can't keep track? Or is it because someone you know has a VA and you want one, too?

By knowing clearly why you want a Virtual Assistant, you automatically are setting the expectation that the person you hire will be able to do those things. If you're wishy-washy about your "why," your VA won't be able to meet your expectations, no matter what they are, because you don't know clearly in your mind what they are.

The bottom line is – if you can't articulate clearly what your reasons are for having a VA, you're not ready. Going into that kind of relationship without a clear vision of what you want the VA to do will only end badly.

The 10 Tips: Setting Expectations

2. Know what your pain points are and how you want the VA to fix them

What's driving you crazy because you can't seem to get to it? This second tip is almost as important as the "why." Here, you need to pinpoint the exact tasks you're looking to have a VA take care of. Again, if you can't articulate what you want the Virtual Assistant to do, you're not ready.

If you're having a problem defining the tasks you want taken care of, it may be because you're not sure exactly what a VA does. Here are just a few of the tasks a VA can take care of, but remember – each VA is different, so you'll need to make sure the VA you're talking to can take care of things the way you want him/her to.

Email management	Calendar management
Travel arrangements	Meeting coordination
Event planning	General writing
Website content creation	Social media management
PowerPoint/presentation creation	Website SEO
Website management	General personal tasks that can be done online (vet appointments, MD appointments, etc)

Does anything in this list make you sit up and say, "Hey! I'd love to have someone take that off my plate, but I can't afford an employee!" If it does, you're in luck. No need for an employee. Just hire a Virtual Assistant that specializes in that area and you'll sleep better at night.

The 10 Tips: Meetings

Everybody hates meetings, even those who organize them. Why? Because so many meetings are just a restatement of something discussed previously, or they turn into a time to yell at employees because they did or did not accomplish something. What a waste.

That's why it's critical to make meetings with your Virtual Assistant productive and not just a rehash of last week's discussion.

Another point: All the expectations of meetings you define for your Virtual Assistant will also work with any meetings you schedule, those with coworkers, others on your same work level, or with your boss. If you're clear here, you can be clear there. And maybe – just maybe – someone will actually stop and say, "Do we really need this meeting?"

3. Know your meeting "why" clearly

Just as with setting expectations, it's critical you know why you want to set a meeting with your Virtual Assistant. Is it to go over what he/she did the previous week? Are you upset about something done or not done? Or are you just setting a regular weekly meeting just because?

By knowing clearly why you want to meet, and the expected result of that meeting, your meetings will accomplish more and will get you both on the same page.

One big no-no about meetings is when you set up a regular weekly meeting as your main means of communicating with your VA. If you're only answering your VA's texts, emails, and phone calls during your meetings, you're handicapping your Virtual Assistant, making it difficult for her to complete the work you've assigned.

The 10 Tips: Meetings

The bottom line is – if you can't articulate clearly what your reasons are for having a meeting, don't schedule the meeting. It'll just waste your time and your VA's time. Besides, regular, weekly meetings that go over the same things week after week are not accomplishing anything.

4. Know what you want to accomplish in the meeting and follow an agenda

You've already gotten a good handle on why you're having a meeting with your Virtual Assistant. Now, you need to put together a cohesive list of items you want to cover during your meeting. Again, if you can't articulate what you want the Virtual Assistant to do, you're not ready to meet.

If you're having a problem defining your agenda, it may be because you're not sure exactly what your goals are or how to reach them. And that's ok – not knowing the "how" can be a line item in your agenda, something for your Virtual Assistant to help you more clearly define in the meeting.

Following an agenda will also ensure you and your Virtual Assistant are on the same page. You'll both be more productive, because your meetings will take less time, and you'll be focused on the same things that need to be accomplished.

One last thing – please don't schedule "regularly-scheduled" meetings, like weekly, monthly, etc. Those meetings, even with agendas, soon turn into talking about the same old stuff, with nothing getting accomplished.

The 10 Tips: Contracts

This may seem to be a simple idea, having a contract when working with a Virtual Assistant, but you'd be surprised at how many relationships in the Gig Economy start off without a contract. It isn't until things go wrong that a contract is drawn up, but, in most cases, it's too late to save the relationship.

5. Not all contracts are created equal

Virtual Assistants have been around for years, but it wasn't until recently that they've been acknowledged as being a profession. Talk to anyone on the street about a VA and a remote executive assistant isn't the first thing that comes to mind.

That being the case, most Virtual Assistants have their own contracts; it's unlikely you have one handy.

A VA contract should include:

- Non-disclosure agreement (covers both you and your clients)

- Pricing (project basis and/or hourly should be spelled out)

- Payment terms (most VAs take PayPal or Stripe, and have very short turnarounds as to when payment is due)

- Work to be performed, either within the contract or as an addendum

- Turnaround times for assigned work and penalties, if any, if work is late

- Termination clause in case of non-payment or other violation of the terms of the contract

The 10 Tips: Contracts

6. Review the contract regularly with your VA

The nature of your work will change as time goes on, especially as it relates to your Virtual Assistant. Different things are assigned to your VA that weren't contemplated in the original contract. Other things have fallen by the wayside. It's even possible your original reason for hiring a VA has changed so dramatically that your VA is doing things far and above what was originally planned.

That being the case, it's important to review your contract regularly, with your Virtual Assistant. Some review the contract monthly, others every six months. Regardless of the timeframe, it's important to make that review session productive.

Don't use the contract review as a time to go over all the things that went wrong since the last contract review; those kinds of grievances should be taken care of quickly, not allowed to fester. The regular contract review should be a time to talk about how much more or less you need of one thing done.

If it's done annually, it's also a good time to talk to your VA about how her pricing has changed. In most cases, your VA won't change your rates, but don't be surprised if it happens. And if the VA is great, go ahead and accept the higher price; he/she is making you look like a star and should be paid accordingly.

The 10 Tips: Negotiating

There are times when you'll need to renegotiate all or part of the contract with your Virtual Assistant. To be successful in your working relationship, there are two areas to which you need to pay special attention – negotiating fairly and negotiating early.

7. Negotiate fairly

At times, your working relationship with your Virtual Assistant is going to need to be changed, as we talked about in Tip 6. The work you do and the work assigned to your VA will more than likely be different than what your original contract said, so it's time to talk about the changes and negotiate a contract change, to be done in writing (which we'll talk about next).

In negotiating fairly, especially if your contracts are reviewed annually, remember that your Virtual Assistant has been there throughout the term of the contract. He/she's made you look good, gotten you better organized, set up and maintained a social media marketing plan, responds quickly to customer complaints – in other words, they've made you look like a star. With that in mind, if your VA says it is time to renegotiate packages or the hourly rate, remember what's been accomplished, not what's been missed. And negotiate fairly

Of course, if a lot of things have been missed, or errors have cost you customers, the time to talk about those items is when they happen, not days/months later.

The 10 Tips: Negotiating

8. Put negotiated changes to the contract in writing

As the relationship with your Virtual Assistant changes over time, and as you've been negotiating changes to the contract, make sure to put those changes in writing as addendums to the contract.

Why is this such a big deal? Because people change, memories fade, relationships grow or fail, and because we can make some mistakes that can't be overlooked. As said in the article "*Get It In Writing: The Importance of Written Agreements in Business*," by Andrew C. Vredenburg, "*A solid written contract can save money and strengthen a business relationship by helping to avoid litigation altogether.*"

Your Virtual Assistant, in her capacity as VA, should take responsibility for documenting your discussion and the agreed-upon contract changes. If he/she doesn't jump at it, task them with it.

Make sure, too, that any changes to the contract are at least e-signed by both parties. There are plenty of e-sign apps and desktop programs available at reasonable prices (free), so there's no excuse not to get it signed off on.

The 10 Tips: Payments

Your Virtual Assistant will typically have a payment portal or a way to accept payments that works for their business. Yet paying for services can shipwreck even the best VA/client relationship.

9. Pay up

As adults, and sometimes even as children, when we perform a job, we expect to be paid for it. One of the first things a new Virtual Assistant does is figure out how to invoice and how to accept payments. Quite a few use PayPal® or Stripe® for electronic payments, while also accepting checks (do people still write checks?).

Your Virtual Assistant has worked hard, doing their best to perform their assigned tasks. There's no reason – NO reason – not to pay an invoice from your VA before or exactly when it's due.

Some will argue they don't have the money on the due date. That's too bad. Most VA contracts spell out when billing is done and the due date when payment is expected. It isn't a surprise. So if you don't have the money to pay your invoice, you shouldn't have taken on a Virtual Assistant to begin with.

The 10 Tips: Payments

Others will say, well, the Virtual Assistant didn't perform the tasks assigned. Also not an excuse for non-payment, especially if billing is on a project basis, with payment due when the project is completed.

For projects, you and your VA should be talking on a regular basis throughout the project, giving you the opportunity to make changes and correct your VA along the way. If you don't take advantage of it, or if you ignore your VA's request for further information or help, that's on you.

So don't be one of those who looks for ways to not pay. Pay what's due, when it's due, without trying to wriggle out of this charge or that charge.

10. Be a superhero

Virtual Assistants run on very lean budgets. Obviously, if you're paying them less than $35/hour, and they're only working for you two hours a day, they're going to have other clients to make up the shortfall. Most VAs are scrupulously honest when billing and have backup to show exactly the number of hours, or proof of a project being completed.

So be a superhero. Surprisingly, all it takes is paying what is due on time, and in the preferred manner.

And it wouldn't hurt if, from time to time, you spend a few dollars and deliver flowers or another kind of bonus, especially if your VA has gone above and beyond expectations.

When Things Go Wrong

You've got your vision and can articulate it clearly. You've signed your virtual assistant's contract, negotiated fairly, and work has started. Everything seems to be going along smoothly. And then it doesn't.

Even with the best intentions on everyone's part, the relationship between you and your VA can break down. Most of the time, it's a simple disagreement that doesn't get fully resolved and is allowed to fester until it blows. Why, though? Why do things go wrong?

From the standpoint of a Virtual Assistant, some of the reasons for derailment include:

- Client doesn't return phone calls
- Client doesn't provide required information to get a task done
- Client isn't answering emails before the task is due

The client may wonder why things don't get done and gets angry with the VA, when, in reality, the client is the reason a task doesn't get resolved.

When Things Go Wrong

What about from the client's standpoint? For the most part, the reasons for complaint by the client are the same:

- The VA doesn't return calls
- The VA doesn't understand a task but doesn't ask questions
- The VA doesn't tell the client of problems that arise

The bottom line when things go wrong is the same – lack of communication. That's why it's so important that both the client (you) and the Virtual Assistant establish and maintain good communications. You don't need to talk every day. You don't need to meet every week. Just establish what works for you, as a team, and maintain it.

One client, the CEO of a media company, and his virtual assistant rarely meet, after two years of working together. In the very beginning, they established that each work better communicating by text. Once the VA got familiar with what needed to be done, managing email and calendaring, she only texted him with questions. He knew she only texted with issues, so he would jump to it when he saw a text from her. They are still working together; he's as organized as he's ever been, loves that she knows when to schedule certain appointments without even asking, and he can go about his business, secure in the knowledge that everything is being taken care of.

Embracing Virtual Assistants in the Gig Economy and the 11th Tip

There's no question the Gig Economy is here to stay. It may evolve over time; most things do. But hiring freelancers and solo entrepreneurs (also known as micro businesses) as Virtual Assistants isn't going anywhere.

When computers first invaded offices back in the 1990s, everyone was sure it meant the end of secretaries and executive assistants. For a while, that did happen, until executives and business owners realized they couldn't manage their own emails and calendars by themselves.

Virtual Assistants are what came out of the reawakening of those in business who finally decided they can't do it all, they need help to carry out the more mundane tasks of business so they can concentrate on the bigger picture of growing their businesses.

These 10 tips for successfully working with a Virtual Assistant were developed after answering the same questions over and over, and watching countless relationships fail between VAs and their clients. Hopefully, more will embrace these 10 tips and develop healthy VA/client relationships that move on through the years, to the benefit of both.

There is an 11th tip, one that doesn't fall within the five areas we talked about – picking the right Virtual Assistant.

There are as many types of Virtual Assistants as there are VAs out there. The work performed by each, along with the personalities, location, culture, and any number of other variables all relate to how a VA works, the type of work performed, how much is charged, and how quickly work can get done.

Before hiring a Virtual Assistant, talk with several. Don't rely on emails and initial interviews. Really talk with them. Get a sense of how they work and what they believe about the work they're doing. And don't choose a VA who focuses mainly on social media when you need someone who manages email and calendaring, and vice versa.

Just as you wouldn't hire a cab driver to pilot an airplane, don't hire the wrong VA just because he/she is the least expensive or the most articulate. Be smart when bringing on your Virtual Assistant and you'll never regret it.

About the Author

Laurie Leiker is an author, freelance writer/editor, Virtual Assistant consultant/coach, and Virtual Assistant.

After working for decades in the medical transcription field, mostly as Director of Operations for several international companies, Laurie found herself at a time in life where working for herself became the best answer to the question, "Kids are grown and out of the house – now what?"

Laurie found the world of Virtual Assistants when looking around for someone to help her with her growing company, hiring her first VA in 2007. Following a fight with breast cancer that took two years and her business, Laurie turned to the field as a way of making ends meet while building her other businesses.

Today, Laurie works with Virtual Assistants and those hiring VAs, as well as working as a freelance writer/editor, and writing books on business, children's books, and a rather clever cookbook, "Frying Solo," recipes for those cooking for one. All Laurie's books can be found on Amazon in both ebook and print forms.

www.ingramcontent.com/pod-product-compliance
Lightning Source LLC
Chambersburg PA
CBHW040350220526
45473CB00009B/2845